Would Y

go on a date to a fancy restaurant that's quite expensive

OR

a cheap restaurant that's quite crowdy?

Would You Rather...

get matching piercings

OR

get matching tattoos?

Would You Rather...

jog in the daytime together

OR

take strolls at night?

Would You Rather...

play your partner's
favorite sport with them

OR

cheer them as they play
it with other people?

Would You Rather...

cuddle by a fireplace

OR

cuddle beside a window?

Would You Rather...

have your lover be
much older

OR

be much younger
than you?

Would You Rather...

your lover be one who likes to dress comfortably

OR

one who likes to dress fashionably?

Would You Rather...

have a partner who wears black all the time

OR

who wears a lot of brightly colored clothes?

Would You Rather...

have a partner who's an extrovert

OR

one who's an introvert?

Would You Rather...

meet your partner's siblings first

OR

their closest friends first?

Would You Rather...

have a partner who
obsessed with hugs
OR
who's obsessed with
cuddles?

Would You Rather...

go shopping for your
significant other alone

OR

go shopping with
their best friend?

Would You Rather...

live on the same street
with your partner
OR
work in the same building
with your partner?

Would You Rather...

have a partner that
always looks nice

OR

a partner that always
smells nice?

Would You Rather...

your partner had really long hair

OR

no hair at all?

Would You Rather...

your partner be one who's very popular on social media

OR

one who's very popular in real life?

Would You Rather...

be with someone who's always really late **OR** who's always really early?

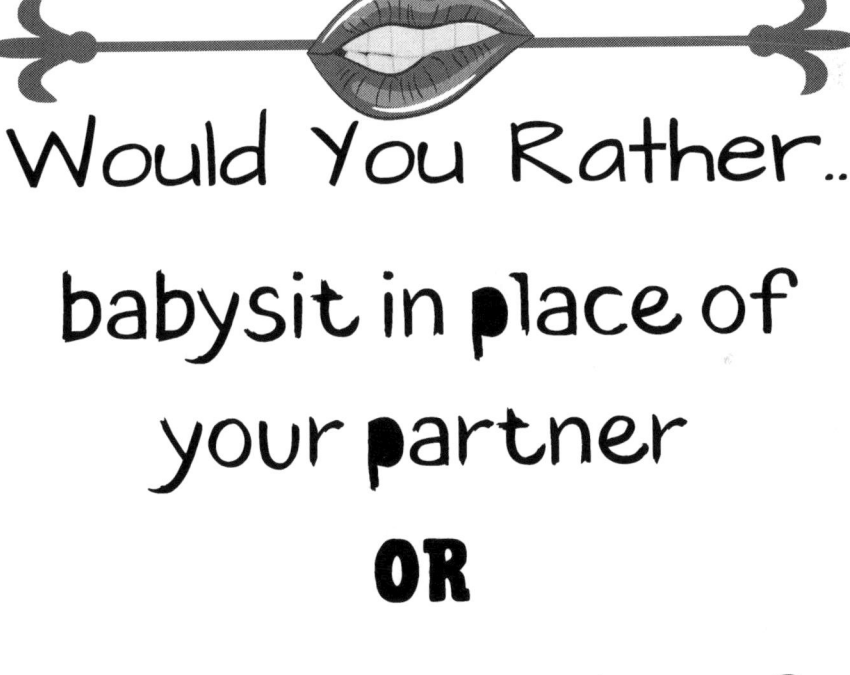

Would You Rather...

babysit in place of your partner **OR** babysit with them?

Would You Rather...

have a partner with an infectious smile
OR
an infectious laugh?

Would You Rather...

video call all day
OR
text each other all night?

Would You Rather...

cook something special for them

OR

have them cook something special for you?

Would You Rather...

have a partner who loves to spend a lot

OR

a partner who loves to save?

Would You Rather... go skydiving with your lover **OR** go mountain climbing?

Would You Rather... give forehead kisses from your partner **OR** get forehead kisses?

Would You Rather...
have a partner
who's a foodie
OR

a partner who hardly ever eats?

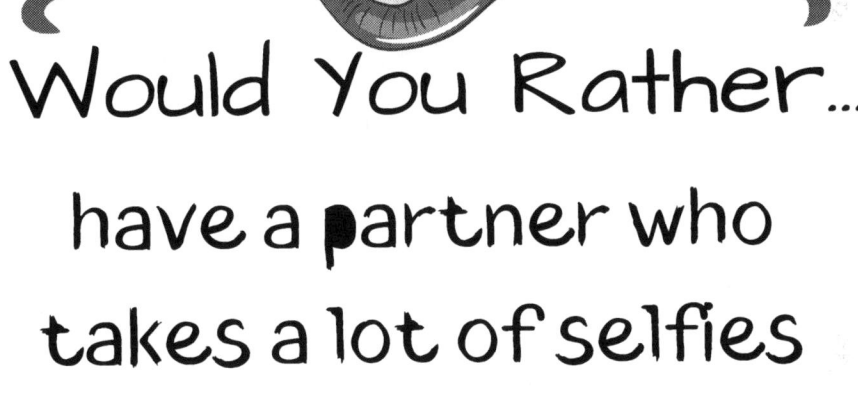

Would You Rather...

have a partner who
takes a lot of selfies

OR

one who takes a lot
of pictures of you?

Would You Rather...

have a partner

who's very funny

OR

a partner who's very

ambitious?

Would You Rather...

have a partner

who's shy

OR

one who makes you

feel shy?

Would You Rather...

earn more than your significant other

OR

have them earn more than you?

Would You Rather...

be with someone who's feared

OR

someone who's loved by all?

Would You Rather...

have a partner who loves
to stay up all night

OR

loves to sleep all day?

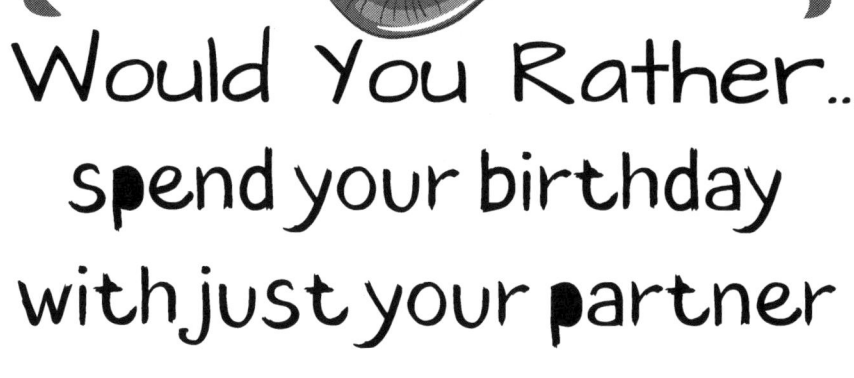

Would You Rather...

spend your birthday
with just your partner

OR

spend it with your partner
and some close friends?

Would You Rather...

have long walks together

OR

take long drives together?

Would You Rather...

give up on your favorite food for three months

OR

not see each other for three months?

Would You Rather...

have a really small wedding with them **OR**

a really big wedding?

Would You Rather...

you both spend the day inside

OR

spend the day outside?

Would You Rather...

go jogging together

OR

go to the gym together?

Would You Rather...

be proposed to in public

OR

be proposed to in private?

Would You Rather...
write love letters for your significant other

OR

write them a song?

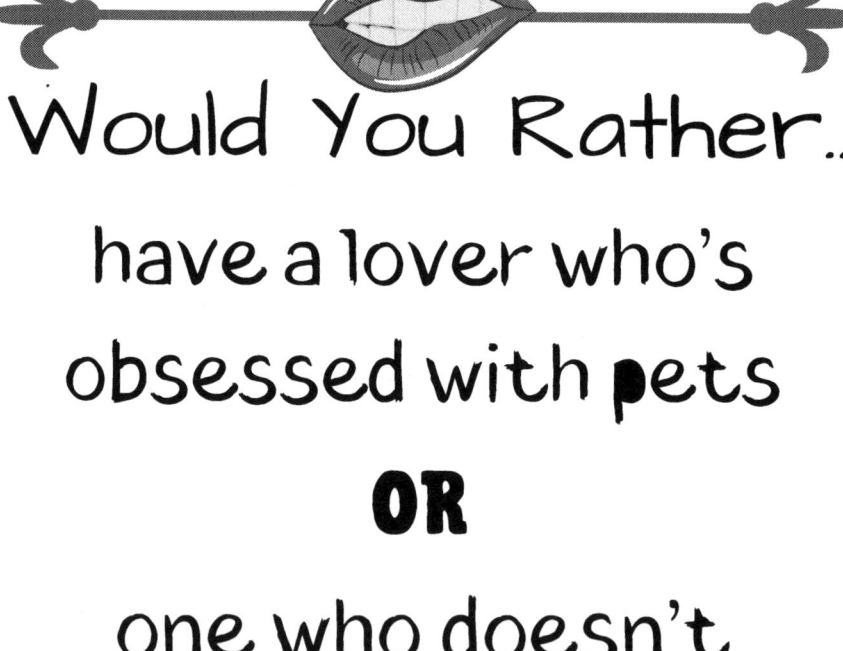

Would You Rather...
have a lover who's obsessed with pets

OR

one who doesn't like pets?

Would You Rather...

be with someone who
eats healthily
OR
who eats whatever they like
but never gains any fat?

Would You Rather...

make a gift by hand for
your partner's birthday
OR
purchase it from a store?

Would You Rather...

our significant other
was an atheist

OR

was a very religious person?

Would You Rather...

go somewhere sunny
for your vacation

OR

go somewhere really cold?

Would You Rather...

have a driver to take
you both around
OR
do the driving by yourself all
the time?

Would You Rather...

give your partner a
foot massage

OR

a back massage?

Would You Rather...

cook something with a lot
of salt for dinner night

OR

cook something with
a lot of **pepper**?

Would You Rather...

build a snowman
together

OR

roll around in the snow
together?

Would You Rather...

have a picnic together early in the morning as the sun rises

OR

late in the evening as the sun sets?

Would You Rather...

get something expensive and precious for your significant other

OR

something cheap but very thoughtful?

Would You Rather...

hold hands in public

OR

Ihave your hands around each other's waists in public?

Would You Rather...

spend the entire day together

OR

have a sleepover at night together?

Would You Rather...

be with someone who knows how to play the instrument

OR

someone who knows how to sing?

Would You Rather...

do karaoke with your partner

OR

watch your partner do karaoke?

Would You Rather...

be with someone with

a lot of class

OR

someone with a lot of

affluence?

Would You Rather...

spend Christmas together

OR

spend new year

together?

Would You Rather...

FaceTime each other

OR

Skype each other?

Would You Rather...

your partner worked
in the army

OR

worked with the navy?

Would You Rather...

have a partner who
uses glasses
OR
a partner who wears
contacts?

Would You Rather...

your partner was
from your hometown

OR

your partner was from
another continent?

Would You Rather...

do some cooking together

OR

do some baking together?

Would You Rather...

find roses all over the house on date night

OR

find scented candles all over the house?

Would You Rather...

report your partner's
wrongdoings to their folks

OR

to their best friend?

Would You Rather...

cuddle up all evening indoors

OR

go watch the sunset
together outside?

Would You Rather...

slow dance to a romantic song together

OR

grind to a fast beat?

Would You Rather...

ride bikes side by side

OR

take long walks side by side?

Would You Rather...

take the most random
selfies with your partner

OR

go to a photo booth?

Would You Rather...

you both went on a date
dressed corporately

OR

dressed casually?

Would You Rather...

go jet-skiing together

OR

go surfing together?

Would You Rather...

go to a musical concert together

OR

go to a drama festival together?

Would You Rather...

share a bottle
of wine together
OR
share the same
glass of wine?

Would You Rather...

eat something exquisite and
different together

OR

eat pizza together?

Would You Rather...

buy them a gift for
valentine's day

OR

make them a gift for
valentine's day?

Would You Rather...

get a tan at the
beach together

OR

go to a tanning salon
together?

Would You Rather...

go partying together

OR

throw a party
at home together?

Would You Rather...

go to an art exhibition
together

OR

do an art exhibition
together?

Would You Rather...

dip your toes in the sand at the beach

OR

draw your initials
in the sand?

Would You Rather...

go for a swim together

OR

relax in a hot tub
together?

Would You Rather...

see your partner in baggy sweatshirts

OR

in a sexy shirt?

Would You Rather...

travel for a living together

OR

travel as a hobby together?

Would You Rather...

your partner owned a jet

OR

owned a yacht?

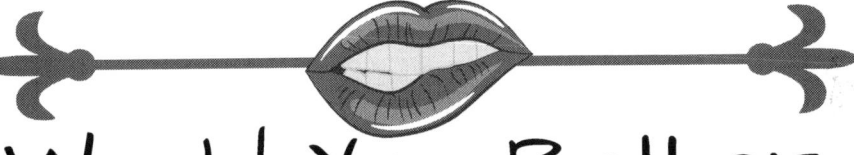

Would You Rather...

your partner was
a science brainiac

OR

one with an artistic soul?

Would You Rather...

your partner has an
excellent sense of smell
OR
an excellent sense
of hearing?

Would You Rather...

your partner drinks only
alcoholic drinks

OR
refuses to touch
anything that isn't
water?

Would You Rather...

your partner had a job that
was life-threatening
OR
a job that took up a lot
of their time?

Would You Rather...

watch Netflix together

OR

watch YouTube videos
together?

Would You Rather...

listen to jazz music
together

OR

listen to blues together?

Would You Rather...

rub your partner's back when
they're sick
OR
rub your partner's
stomach when they're
sick?

Would You Rather...

be with someone who works from home

OR

someone who goes to the office every morning?

Would You Rather...

get lots of forehead kisses

OR

lots of kisses on the cheeks?

Would You Rather...

go to a formal event together

OR

go to a casual event together?

Would You Rather...

your partner was one that laughs a lot

OR

one that makes you laugh a lot?

Would You Rather...

be with a chef

OR

be with a foodie?

Would You Rather...

have your honeymoon
somewhere popular and fancy

OR

somewhere unknown and
very homely?

Would You Rather...

your partner had blue eyes

OR

brown eyes?

Would You Rather...

wear matching leather boots

OR

matching sneakers?

Would You Rather...

be with someone who
stares at you a lot
OR
one who loves to have your
attention all the time?

Would You Rather...

read a book together

OR

listen to an audiobook
together?

Would You Rather...

buy a penthouse together

OR

buy a beach house together?

Would You Rather...

live in a town together

OR

live in a city together?

Would You Rather...

roll on your significant other

OR

roll off the bed?

Would You Rather...

be with someone really skinny

OR

someone really huge?

Would You Rather...

wear your significant
other's underwear

OR

go out with no underwear?

Would You Rather...

your significant other looked
like a child

OR

acted like a child?

Would You Rather...

press a zit on your significant
other's face
OR
watch someone else do it?

Would You Rather...

cuddle for five minutes

OR

cuddle for five hours?

Would You Rather...

have a partner who talks to their dog

OR

who "listens" to their dog talk?

Would You Rather...

have met much later in life

OR

much earlier in life?

Would You Rather...

your lover took a vow of celibacy all of a sudden

OR

took a vow of silence all of a sudden?

Would You Rather...

watch a badly scripted movie together

OR

watch a comedy together?

Would You Rather...

your partner didn't brush
for a week

OR

didn't shower for a week?

Would You Rather...

have a partner who eats
really fast in public

OR

one who chews really
noisily in public?

Would You Rather...

find out your partner just gave birth to a baby

OR

has twins from their last relationship?

Would You Rather...

your partner had a much bigger head

OR

a much smaller head?

Would You Rather...

your partner had a house
that looked bad
OR

a house that smelt bad?

Would You Rather...

your partner was the richest
garbage man in the world

OR

the poorest banker in the
world?

Would You Rather...

have a partner with a really squeaky voice

OR

one with a crooked voice?

Would You Rather...

have a very mischievous partner

OR

have a very boring partner?

Would You Rather...

be with someone who's very lazy and dirty

OR

someone who's a clean freak?

Would You Rather...

your partner was always overdressed to places

OR

was always underdressed?

Would You Rather...

have a partner who likes to scream
and throw a tantrum when upset

OR

a partner who easily breaks down
and starts to cry when upset?

Would You Rather...

be with someone who snores
really loudly when asleep

OR

someone who sleeps like a
dead person?

Would You Rather...

be with a computer geek

OR

be with someone who has no idea
on how to use technology?

Would You Rather...

your partner was really hairy

OR

didn't have a single hair on
them?

Would You Rather...

you bend down to kiss your significant other because of their height
OR
stand on your tiptoe to kiss your significant other?

Would You Rather...

your partner was really tall and chubby

OR

your partner was really short and trim looking?

Would You Rather...

your partner looked weak but
was actually really strong

OR

looked strong but was actually
really weak?

Would You Rather...

have quadruplets with
your partner

OR

have twins?

Would You Rather...

your partner was a
millionaire but a moron

OR

was really broke but a genius?

Would You Rather...

have a partner who
never shaves

OR

a partner who never uses
deodorant?

Would You Rather...

be with someone with
a fat tummy

OR

someone with a hairy tummy?

Would You Rather...

have pillow fights together

OR

food fights?

Would You Rather...

kiss your partner after
they ate a full garlic

OR

after they told you they hadn't
brushed in a week?

Would You Rather...

dance together
under the sun

OR

under the rain?

Would You Rather...

be with someone who
snores loudly

OR

who talks in their sleep?

Would You Rather...

have a partner who sings
in the shower

OR

who sings while on the
toilet seat?

Would You Rather...

be with someone who always eats with their hands

OR

someone who doesn't know how to use a fork and a knife?

Would You Rather...

be with someone with zero fashion sense

OR

someone with an outdated fashion sense?

Would You Rather...

be with someone who laughs really loudly

OR

someone who laughs really weirdly?

Would You Rather...

steal your partner's shirt

OR

steal your partner's shorts?

Would You Rather...

wear your partner's
underwear

OR

wear your dirty underwear?

Would You Rather...

tickle your partner till they
start to laugh hysterically

OR

tickle them till they start
to cry?

Would You Rather...

date a comedian

OR

date a clown?

Would You Rather...

have a partner with
horrible dancing skills

OR

one who's too hyper when
they dance?

Would You Rather...

be with someone who
smells funny

OR

someone who likes
to smell you?

Would You Rather...

draw a mustache over your
partner's face when
they're asleep

OR

rub lipstick all over their
mouth when they're
asleep?

Would You Rather...

try on your partner's clothes

OR

have your partner try on your clothes?

Would You Rather...

lick your partner all over

OR

kiss your partner all over?

Would You Rather...

be with someone who
eats a lot
OR
someone who plays
with their food?

Would You Rather...

sit on your partner to
prevent them from leaving
OR
tie your partner to
prevent them from
leaving?

Would You Rather...

die for your lover

OR

have a lover who's willing
to die for you?

Would You Rather...

get the silence treatment

OR

hurl words at each other
when upset?

Would You Rather...

your partner was one who turned
everything into a competition

OR

one who was a sore loser?

Would You Rather...

find a soul mate and have all
your friends hate him

OR

find a soul mate that
hates all your friends?

Would You Rather...

let your partner go through
your WhatsApp texts
OR
go through your Facebook
messenger texts?

Would You Rather...

have a partner who never
has your time

OR

a partner who's
quite clingy?

Would You Rather...

your partner had a tattoo with
the initials of his ex-wife

OR

his ex-girlfriend?

Would You Rather...

get married and never
have kids

OR

have kids and never
get married?

Would You Rather...

your partner loved your friends
and hated your family

OR

loved your family and
hated your friends?

Would You Rather...

see your partner only on
the weekdays but at work

OR

only on the weekends
at home?

Would You Rather...

be with a soldier

OR

be with a terrorist?

Would You Rather...

still be in contact
with your ex

OR

find out your significant other
was still in contact with their ex?

Would You Rather...

lose all your selfies

OR

lose all your pictures with your significant other?

Would You Rather...

your partner drove a rickety car

OR

your partner didn't have a car at all?

Would You Rather...

be with someone that
talks a lot

OR

someone who likes to keep
things bottled up inside?

Would You Rather...

be with someone
who's very proud

OR

someone with low
self-esteem?

Would You Rather...

commit a crime with
your lover

OR

turn your lover in for a crime
they committed?

Would You Rather...

your partner's
mother didn't like you

OR

your partner's father
didn't like you?

Would You Rather...

serve burnt food for

you both to eat

OR

half-cooked food for you both

to eat?

Would You Rather...

have a partner who

thinks a lot

OR

a partner who could never

think for their self?

Would You Rather...

have a partner who's antisocial

OR

a partner who likes to be friends with everyone?

Would You Rather...

have a partner who gets jealous all the time

OR

a partner who makes you jealous all the time?

Would You Rather...

watch a horror movie together

OR

watch a tragedy movie together?

Would You Rather...

get a terrible gift for your birthday

OR

no gift at all?

Would You Rather...

be with someone who's a vegetarian
OR
someone who's trying to get you to be a vegetarian?

Would You Rather...

your partner dumped you

OR

you dumped your partner?

Would You Rather...

watch your partner dance
with someone else
OR
dance with your partner, even
though you suck at it?

Would You Rather...

meet your partner's
parents first
OR
have your partner meet your
parents first?

Would You Rather...

you both worked in the same
office but earn peanuts

OR

work in different countries
and earn seven digit salaries?

Would You Rather...

your partner had a lot of
friends of the opposite gender

OR

they had no friends at all?

Would You Rather...

be with someone who has to
go to bed late every night

OR

one who has to get up early
every morning?

Would You Rather...

your partner was a celebrity
with a lot of money but fans of
the opposite sex

OR

your partner was
unsuccessful and broke?

Would You Rather...

live in a slum with your significant other

OR

move into a decent place alone?

Would You Rather...

abandon your partner to suffer the consequences of their sins

OR

suffer with your partner?

Would You Rather...

your partner worked for an ex
they broke up with
OR
worked for someone who hurt
them the past?

Would You Rather...

have a partner who was always
stressed at work
OR
a partner who constantly
brings home all the stress of
the day to pour it out on you?

Would You Rather...

be with someone who's always
on their phone

OR

someone who's always going
through your phone?

Would You Rather...

date someone who likes to
stay alone a lot

OR

someone who enjoys the
company of people a lot?

Would You Rather...

be failures together

OR

go your separate ways and
become very successful?

Would You Rather...

lie to them to protect
their feelings

OR

tell them the truth and hurt
their feelings?

Would You Rather...

share some bad news with your partner
OR

have them find out at a later date on their own?

Would You Rather...

have a partner who messes up the toilet occasionally

OR

one who flares up at the slightest mess they notice in the toilet?

Would You Rather...

your partner was broke and didn't tell anyone

OR

your partner was broke and told only a close friend of the opposite sex?

Would You Rather...

your partner broke an arm

OR

broke a leg?

Would You Rather...

your partner had a terrible addiction they couldn't drop **OR**

your partner had a terrible addiction that they refused to believe was bad?

Would You Rather...

have a significant other who was too romantic and sweet **OR**

one who didn't know how to be romantic and sweet?

Would You Rather...

your partner was an extremely
rich person doing a shady business

OR

a wretched person in
a legal profession?

Would You Rather...

be accused of stealing a
lady's underwear

OR

discover that the toilet is broken after
taken a very discomforting poo in your
crush's house?

Would You Rather...

French kiss your partner when they have oral herpes

OR

French kiss your significant other when they have bleeding sores?

Would You Rather...

be accused of stealing a lady's underwear

OR

discover that the toilet is broken after taken a very discomforting poo in your crush's house?

Manufactured by Amazon.ca
Bolton, ON

14570186R00057